1. Redcliff Hill, with St. Mary Redcliff Church and the Shot Tower middle distance, where lead shot was made by dropping the lead from inside the top of the tower, an idea developed by William Watts, in 1782. The tower and rank of adjoining shops were demolished for road widening in 1968. The postcard was posted in 1912.

C. E. H. COLLARD, 94 REDCLIFT HILL, BRISTOL, MARCH 16TH 1905.

2. Collard's the butchers, Mr and Mrs Collard standing outside their shop, with two members of their staff in 1905. The postcard, written by C.E.H. Collard to a Mr Benson of Southville, was asking him to please "call and oblige".

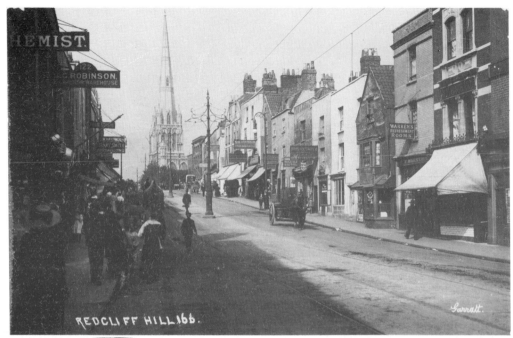

3. A superb photographic postcard from the bottom of Redcliff Hill, showing the many varied shops, and the spire of St. Mary Redcliff Church, with the famous Faggott and Pea Shop on the right. Picture by Garratt, before 1914.

4. This view of Redcliff Hill, taken from Bedminster Bridge, shows the tram lines and the ornate poles in the centre of the road. The postcard was posted in 1912.

5. Bedminster Bridge showing the ornate ironwork of the bridge, with the river flowing beneath. Next door to the George and Dragon Public House is the Redcliff Almhouses. This view was taken before 1910.

6. Another view in the same direction from Bedminster Bridge, a tram almost opposite the junction with Commercial Road. Many advertisements on the hoardings include such names as Oxo, Robin Starch, and Wills Capstan Cigarettes, 10 for 6d, 20 for 11½d.

7. Looking towards Bedminster Bridge, from the iron railing in York Road, the tower of Bristol General Hospital beyond the bridge. The postcard was posted in 1912.

8. York Road, the three-storied houses facing the river, nos. 4-20, near Bedminster Bridge. Note the three faces at the upstairs window, and the boys with their home-made trolley.

9. Bedminster Parade, also known as The Causeway, shows Bristol Free Library on the left dating around 1877, and the square tower of the then Bedminster Police Station beyond. This view posted in 1905.

10. Looking in the opposite direction showing the whole front of the Police Station, with the clock in the tower. The postcard was posted in 1910.

11. The offices of the Imperial Tobacco Company nearing completion in 1908, on the corner of Lombard Street and East Street. The scaffolding was erected by the Bristol Wire Rope Co., using improved flexible steel wire, with scaffolding lashes.

12. The completed Wills' offices, with its imposing round tower, taken a few years later than picture 11, in 1913.

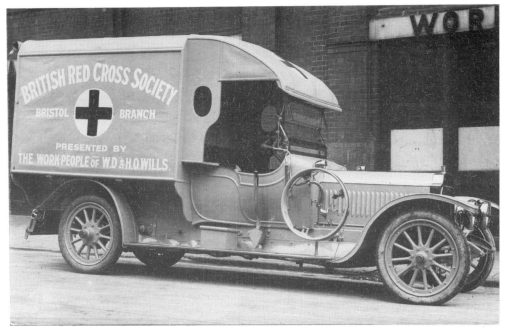

**13.** The ambulance presented to the British Red Cross Society, paid for by the contributions from the workers of W.D. & H.O. Wills during the 1914-18 war. Note the handbrake on the outside of the drivers door.

**14.** This view shows the new Bedminster Library, which was opened in 1913. It was built on the site of the Temperance Hall, replacing the Free Library, which was situated further along Bedminster Parade, adjoining Bedminster Police Station.

**15.** East Street, also known as Bedminster Parade, as this card suggests, a thriving shopping area, with many of their customers workers from W.D. & H.O. Wills. Card postally used in 1925, and published by Chatterton.

**16.** Looking along East Street with part of the Wills' Cigarette Factory on the right, four loading bays under the famous Wills' clock, a Mardon's horse drawn delivery wagon parked outside the factory, about 1911.

17. Bedminster Hippodrome in East Street in its hey day in the 1920's. The Hippodrome was opened in 1911 as a theatre, changing to silent films in 1915. It was bombed in 1941, and the remains were pulled down for a shop to be built in 1954.

18. Looking along East Street showing the varied shops, towards Bedminster Hippodrome, the junction for Mill Lane opposite the tram. The card was posted on 20th April 1920.

19. This view is along East Street, in 1915, before the old properties covered in advertising hoardings were demolished, behind the tram. The tram was advertising the Bristol Tramways and Carriage Company, private motor cars for hire.

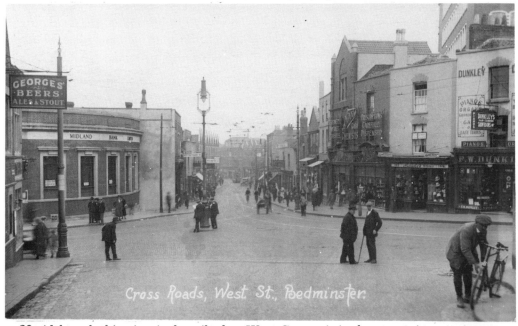

20. Although this view is described as West Street, it is the same view as picture 19, but 10 years later in 1925. The Midland Bank is now on the corner of East Street and Cannon Street.

21. Tram no. 84 from Cannon Street is about to turn into East Street, the pointed roof of the London Inn behind. Tram no. 99 passing in the opposite direction, toward Ashton. The card was posted in Bristol in 1918.

22. A closer view of the Bedminster Tram Depot, with tram no. 26 just passing the turning for St. Johns Road, with the lower windows of the Robinsons' factory to the left of the tram depot, now owned by Cameron Balloons. The tram depot was bombed at 6 a.m. on January 4th 1941. This view was taken in 1939.

23. West Street in the direction of Bedminster and the centre of the city about 1910. The Pawnbrokers sign of three golden balls is by the tram stop. The Jolly Collier Public House is on the bend centre distance.

24. West Street from outside the Jolly Collier, the tram enroute for Bedminster Down, a lively scene, postcard taken from the same series as picture 23, about 1910.

**25.** West Street looking towards the tram depot, and the corner of E.S. & A. Robinsons' factory. The Sportsmans Arms, and advertising hoardings. Delightful groups of children are wandering quite safely across the road. The postcard was posted in May 1913 and published by Viner.

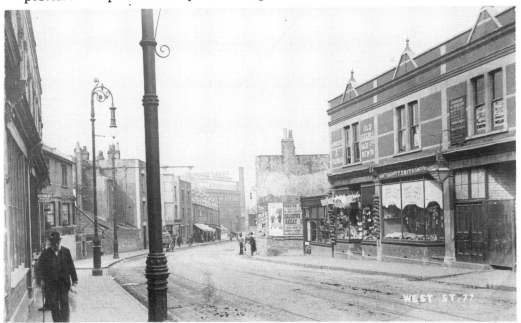

**26.** In the same direction in West Street, Robinsons' factory can still be seen. Shops include G. Steinburg ironmongers, and advertises old couches made like new 8/6d (42½p).

27. West Street, a funeral procession wending its way past the junction with Diamond Street. The shop on the corner owned by Hurditch, harness and saddle maker.

28. From the beginning of Bedminster Down Road, towards West Street, with the junction of Parson Street to the right, and the old Toll House built in 1727. Tram no. 100 enroute for Bristol Bridge from Bedminster Down. The postcard was posted in 1919.

29. The Luckwell Hotel, on the corner of Luckwell Road and Palmyra Road. The then proprietor W.J. Hamlyn. This delightful view from before 1910 shows horse and coach, and carriage, the only transport, and people gathered for a days outing.

30. Luckwell Road is a long road, which connects with North Street, and at Winterstoke Road the other end. This view is typical of the double bay villas in the road. This postcard was posted in 1908.

COPYRIGHT AFS. BL. 51.     CORONATION ROAD, BRISTOL.

**31.** The beginning of Coronation Road from the Bedminster end, the elegant three-storey houses facing the river in this view in March 1934, with St. Pauls Church in the distance.

Coronation Road, Southville.

30
PHOTO
HEPWORTH.

**32.** A closer view of St. Pauls Church, showing the varied architecture in Coronation Road. This postcard was published by Hepworth, and posted in 1934.

"BRISTOL'S OWN" (and others) at Bedminster Y.M.C.A., February 12th, 1915.

33. The Y.M.C.A, the initials of Young Men's Christian Association, was first formed in Bristol in 1853. The Bedminster branch opened in premises in East Street in April 1904, but was only open in the evenings. This war-time view in 1915 shows soldiers and local people at a patriotic event.

34. The correct name for Walton Road, as on this postcard, is Walton Street, a turning off Sheene Road. The church tower of St. Johns is behind the houses. This card was published by E.C. Stevens, and posted in Bristol in 1910.

**35.** The Goal Ferry Bridge under construction in September 1935. It was built as a connecting footbridge between Cumberland Road and Coronation Road, displacing the ferry which is still in use in the picture.

**36.** The same footbridge now complete taken from Coronation Road. The uneven footpath and slipway of the former ferry showing on the Cumberland Road side. The postcard was posted in October 1936.

37. Stackpool Road before 1910, a house to let on the left, and many pot-hole puddles in the road. The road connects with Dean Lane.

38. Greville Road, a long road leading off of North Street. This view is taken about 1910.

**39.** Coronation Road, named after King George IV, as his Coronation was being celebrated when the road was opened, in 1822. The opening ceremony performed by Dowager Lady Smyth who lived at Clift House, which at that time was the Dower House of the Smyth's of Ashton Court.

**40.** Coronation Road about 1906. The trees and railings by the river known as the 'cut' showing on the right. This waterway was started in 1804 at Wapping, by French prisoners, and water from the Avon flowed into the new bed in 1909.

41. This view of Coronation Road, written from no. 164 on July 15th 1908, the message mentions they have just moved in, and were in a bit of a muddle! The baker can be seen with his delivery basket by the ornate lamp standard.

J. BAWN, Cab Proprietor & Furniture Remover, 1. Beauly Rd., Southville, Bristol.
Tel. 2677X                                                    Estimates Free.

42. J. Bawn cab proprietor and furniture remover of Beauly Road, off of Coronation Road. This hansom cab available for hire. Note the early telephone number.

**43.** Beauley Road, with St. Davids Church on the corner with Park Road. The general shop on the opposite corner with Raleigh Road. The postcard was posted in 1918, and published by Viner of Bath.

**44.** Park Road. The road looking towards Camden Road from Beauley Road. This is an early view posted from Bristol in 1907.

**45.** Pearl Street, a turning from South Street off the main road — North Street. One of several streets in the area named after precious stones. C. Matthews, Decorator and Paperhanger, is the sign on the house on the left of the card, in about 1906.

**46.** Islington Road leads to Allington Road, just off of Coronation Road. Two little girls warmly dressed, standing for the camera. This postcard, dated 1906, is one of many views taken in the same series.

**47.** Pembroke Road. Single bay villas lead to Stackpool Road. This card posted on November 19th 1906, to Keynsham. Note the spelling on the card.

**48.** Fairfield Road, a turning off the main road, North Street. The double bay villas featuring lace curtains and slat-blinds, which were popular in the mid 1906 period.

49. Southville U.M. Church on the corner of Howard Road, not far from Coronation Road.

50. Merrywood School on the corner of Stackpool and Merrywood Roads. The girls in neat gym slips, are holding sticks for a team event.

51. This group of young children are with their nannies. They are dependant on gifts of money and parcels to support the children. The postcard was sent by one of the staff thanking a Mrs Leggett for her parcel in March 1914.

52. The staff of Ashton Gate Junior School, taken on Peace Day, July 24th 1919. Rather serious expressions for a Celebration Day!

53. Taken from Bedminster Station looking towards St. Pauls Church on the skyline, and the E.S. & A. Robinson printing factory. Hereford Street, the road in the centre, is leading in the direction of East Street.

54. The Bristol Co-operative Society float for a parade advertising their bakery and confectionery department, taken below the open space in Sheene Road, near the Malago Stream.

55. St. Johns Lane, before the houses were built opposite Victoria Park Primary School. This postcard was posted on April 4th 1906.

56. Windmill Hill Schools, Victoria Park, built on the borders of Victoria Park facing the G.W.R. railway line to the South West. This card was published by Viners of Weston and Bath in November 1916.

57. Chessil Street, quite a long road between Luckwell Road, crossing Jasper Street and connecting with West Street. Children gathered in the road on this postcard from before 1910.

58. Nutgrove Avenue faces the south west side of Victoria Park and joins with Hill Avenue. A summers day, with two men in their straw boater hats.

VICTORIA PARK BEDMINSTER.

59. Victoria Park. The park keeper standing inside the iron fencing around shrubs and flower beds. Windmill Hill School on the left, and houses on the slopes of Totterdown in the distance on the right. The card was posted in 1921, but the photograph was taken a few years earlier.

Hill Avenue, Victoria Park, Bristol. 54

60. Hill Avenue, Victoria Park, between St. Lukes Road and Almorah Road. This view shows the Almorah Road end, quite a wide thoroughfare in 1913.

**61.** St. Michaels and All Angels Church and vicarage, built in 1886. Groups of children are standing for the photographer. This postcard was posted in 1908.

**62.** Victoria Park looking towards the city. The spire of St. Mary Redcliff Church showing between the trees. The railway line of the G.W.R. runs across the foreground, with Pylle Hill Goods Depot bottom right.

**63.** H.C. Hills household supply shop at 115-117 North Street, on the corner of Dorset Street, outside are the staff, Eileen Garland, Arthur — , with Manager George Croome. The picture was taken in 1930. The premises were destroyed in an air raid during the 1940-45 war.

**64.** H.C. Hills delivery van, registration number HT 4989, before 1920. The driver in the trilby is William Claridge. Their deliveries extended to the districts of Knowle West, Brislington, Shirehampton, and Long Ashton. The bell hanging at the top of the door was rung to draw attention to the delivery van arriving with calls of "Oil, Oil".

**65.** North Street cinema on the junction with Raleigh Road, opened in 1912. Later changing its name to the Plaza. Raleigh Road Post Office is situated next door but one to the cinema.

**66.** North Street was a busy shopping area with quite a variation of architecture. A sign for Willways Dye Works is on the left and a bread delivery cart is on its rounds.

**67.** Looking along North Street in the opposite direction from picture no. 65, the Imperial Tobacco Factory of Franklyn Davey & Co. is seen on the corner of Raleigh Road. A tram is enroute for Bristol Bridge from Ashton Gate.

**68.** North Street in the opposite direction to picture no. 67. Lime Street is the turning by Scotts Store. This postcard was published by Viner, and posted in 1930 to the United States of America.

69. Birch Road, an uninterrupted view taken in 1906. The road connects with Raleigh Road and Vicarage Road.

Raleigh Road, Southville. 727.

70. Raleigh Road in the direction of Beauley Road. The church of St. Davids and the prominant premises of Bedminster Co-operative Society are seen middle distance.

71. Frayne Road, facing Ashton Park, looking towards one of the Tobacco Bond Warehouses built between 1906-1919 at the Cumberland Basin.

72, A game of bowls in Ashton Park, with Frayne Road facing the green. The postcard was sent from 26 Frayne Road, and the message reads "..the name of the vacuum cleaner is 'The Gem' 30/6d (£1.52½)!" It was posted in February 1910.

73. A parade of soldiers recruited for service in the Army during the 1914-18 war. St. Francis' Church behind the hoardings was built in 1891. The vicarage beyond survives today although the church was destroyed in 1941 and has since been rebuilt.

74. Ashton Park children outside the seated shelter in June 1923, when this postcard was sent. The top of one of the Tobacco Bond Warehouses can just be seen above the pointed roof of the shelter.

**75.** A bustling scene in Upton Road, dominated by the Imperial Tobacco Factories either side of the road. The Cricketers Arms public house is beyond the high walls of the factory.

**76.** The Vauxhall Footbridge from the Cumberland Road side of the river, towards Coronation Road. The swinging of the bridge let a tug through. The postcard was posted in October 1910.

77. The Round House, with its rounded porch at the junction with Coronation Road and North Street. One of a series of cards produced before 1914.

78. A closer view of the Round House, showing the latticed windows, and adverts either side. Advertising Ashton Gate Breweries, North Street. The Imperial Tobacco Factory dominating the view.

79. Tram no.82 passing the Round House. This view is further along Ashton Road, with the wall and trees in Ashton Park on the left and various shops with an advert for Singers Sewing Machines above one of the shops. The postcard was posted in 1918.

80. Looking in the opposite direction to picture 79, the lamp standard has a sign directing to Bedminster, one mile, and towards the park Weston-Super-Mare. Postcard by Viner of Bath.

BATTEN. T. GALE. W. RIPPON. R. YOUNG. W. DEMMERY. A. SPEAR. MR. BACON. MR. THICKETT.
TRAINER. DIRECTOR. MANAGER.
C R. MARR. F. W. STAINFORTH. W. P. MAXWELL. GILLIGAN. F. CONNOLLY. P. HANLIN. J. COTTLE. MR. DEVERIDGE.
DIRECTOR.
RAPID PHOTO E C. W. WEDLOCK. F. HILTON.

81. Bristol City Football Team in the 1907-08 season. They are seen here with their trainer, Mr. Batten, Manager, Mr. Thickett, and Director, Mr. Bacon. One of their most famous and long serving players W. Wedlock, is sat left in the front row. He was known as Billy "Fatty" Wedlock. In the 1920-21 season it was his testimonial year, by that time he had won 28 medals, and 19 full caps.

82. The Bristol City Ground was used for many celebration events over the years. One of the highlights was on Empire Day, when school children paraded and performed. This postcard was taken in 1911.

**83.** Crowds swarming over the newly completed Ashton Swing Bridge in 1906. The signal box was for use on the railway line, underneath the road bridge, and on the right the brick wall of one of the Tobacco Bond Warehouses.

**84.** A view of the Ashton Swing Bridge from the river, showing clearly the railway line and road bridge above, with children standing on the muddy banks. Postally used in 1913.

85. Ashton Gate Halt opened in 1906 on the Bristol-Portishead line, to serve the football crowds at Bristol City Ground, at Ashton Gate. On the line to the right, a saddle tank engine, with the Clifton Suspension Bridge on the skyline.

86. Ashton Avenue in the direction of Cumberland Basin, the Tobacco Bonds and Ashton Swing Bridge. A wide road for 1913, and a horse and cart with the driver standing in the middle of the road!

# INDEX

**A**
Ashton Ave 86
Ashton Cinema 65
Ashton Gate Halt 85
Ashton Gate Junior School 52
Ashton Park 72, 74
Ashton Road 80
Ashton Swing Bridge 83, 84

**B**
Bawn Cab Proprietor 42
Beauley Road 43
Bedminster Bridge 5, 6, 7
Bedminster Church and Parish 53
Bedminster Down Road 28
Bedminster Hippodrome 17
Bedminster Library 14
Bedminster Parade 10, 15
Birch Road 69
Bristol City F.C. 81
Bristol City Ground 82
British Red Cross Ambulance 13

**C**
Causeway 9
Chessel Street 57
Coronation Road 31, 32, 39, 40, 41
Creche 51

**E**
East Street 16, 18, 19, 20

**F**
Frayne Road 71
Fairfield Road 48

**G**
Goal Ferry Bridge 35, 36
Greville Road 38

**H**
Hill Avenue 60
Hills Delivery Van 64
Hills Shop 63

**I**
Imperial Tobacco Co. 11, 12
Islington Road 46

**L**
London Inn 21
Luckwell Hotel 29
Luckwell Road 30

**M**
Merrywood School 50

**N**
North Street 66, 67, 68, 73
Nutgrove Ave 58

**P**
Park Road 44
Pearl Street 45
Pembroke Road 47

**R**
Raleigh Road 70
Redcliff Hill 1, 2, 3, 4
Round House 77, 78, 79

**S**
Stackpool Road 37
Southville U.M. Church 49
Sheene Road 54
St. Johns Lane School 55
St. Michael and All Angels Church 61

**U**
Upton Road 75

**V**
Vauxhall Bridge 76
Victoria Park 59, 62

**W**
Walton Street 34
West Street 22, 23, 24, 25, 26, 27
Windmill Hill School 56

**Y**
York Road 8
Y.M.C.A. 33